for you, the world.

subh

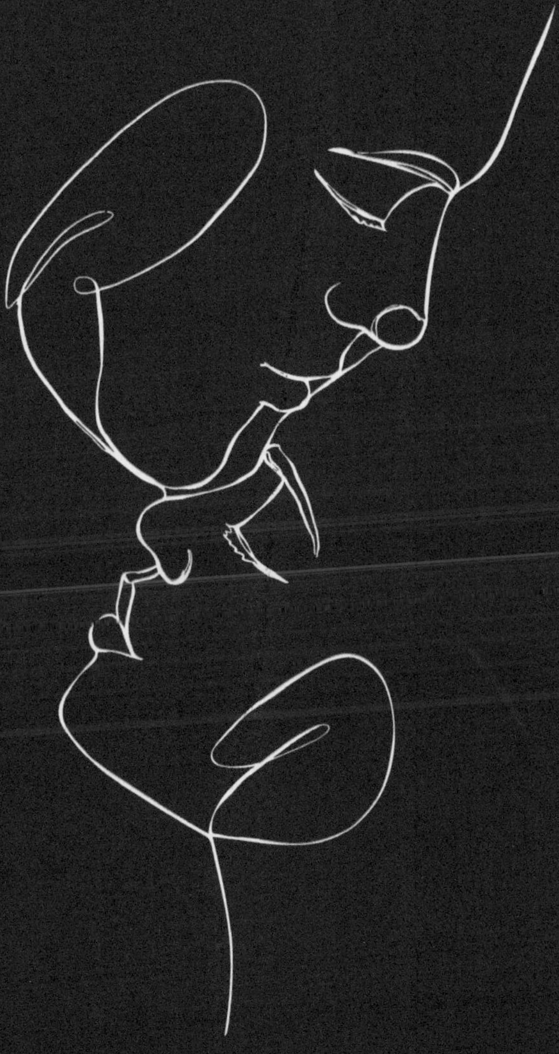

to: him

i love you to you and back

i will endure a lifetime of missing you for the privilege of being loved by you.

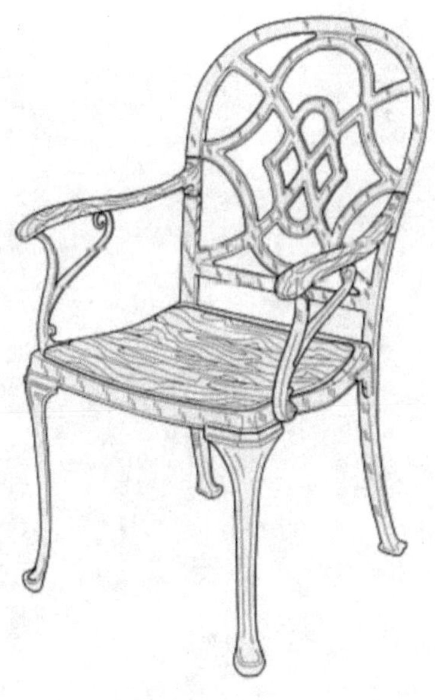

CHAPTERS:

how can i kill myself for another,
when i'm *still dying* for you?

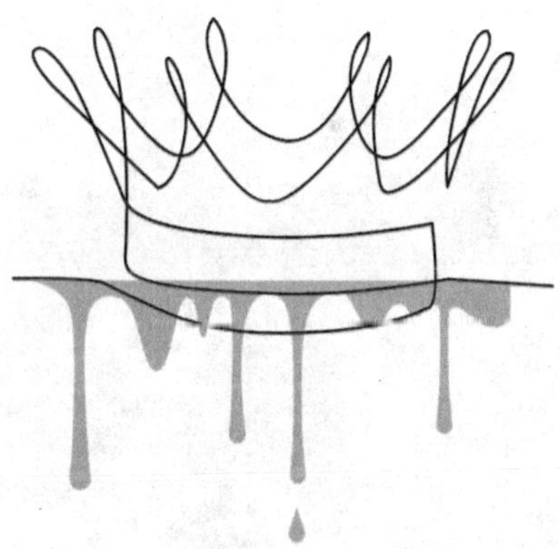

shame

for once i wish you showed me
that you cared about my bleeding wound,
not that it was staining your shirt.

i often question if you were happy
or if you simply stayed because you knew that i was.

living without you is to be blessed with a curse
where i can breathe,
but not live.

what felt like the end,
could just be the end of a chapter,
one of many.

there's more to our story
i promise.

one day we will come back to this page
but that time
we will finish our story.

-at least i hope

i hate that the two young lovers we once were
will never get to see the happy ending
they fought hand, tooth, and nail to live.

it still burns,
the thought that we were meant to be,
but are no longer.

i still go to sleep every night
with stories to tell you,
only to remember that you are gone.
i now suffer grieving someone
that still walks this earth,
although they are no longer holding my hand
throughout their journey.

right person wrong time
felt like such an injudicious fallacy
until i met you.

for how was it truly possible
to be so helpless
yet ardent.

the countless amount of hours i'd spend
praying,
repenting,
pleading,

to whoever could possibly fulfil my nonsensical plea,
to one day feel the grace of your embrace once again,
or simply to be with you once more.

if there is a next time,
i pray we love one another
in languages we won't have to
spend eternity transcribing.

i spoke to the moon tonight,
she asked about you,
questioning whether it was too good to be true,
or if stories like ours were truly lived,
or were they merely reveries,
that took their promenade within the human mind.

i stood silent,
there were simply no words to adhere to her curiosity.

minutes passed,
minutes turned into hours,
hours turned into what felt like days,

yet my thoughts remained desolate.

what words were there to adequately elucidate
how everything was perfect with you
at least it felt like it was
and that's all that really mattered.

if you ever feel lost,
remember that i will always be waiting,
even if i am no longer your home.

it was as if you were from a past life,
for no stranger would have made it
this difficult to stop myself from looking back

whenever i go silent
they ask me if i'm thinking of you,
for whenever i do talk
your name is the only utterance that my lips
wish to voice.

i'm afraid i'll feel most alive
when i perish,
for the smallest part of me
still believes death will be the next phase to our potential
eternity.

"nobody stays forever"
you screamed.
i'll be nobody.
i still am screaming, if you care to listen.

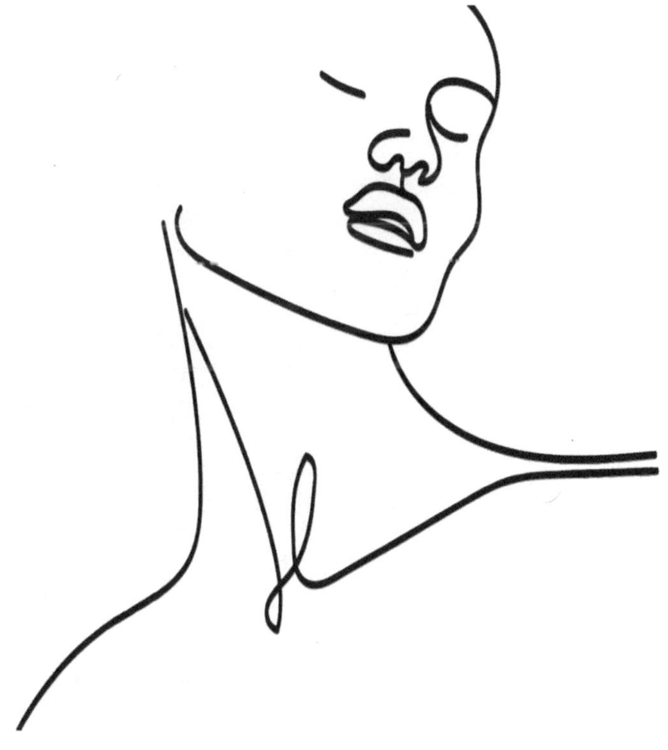

the saddest part,
was realising that we truly could've made it work,
you just weren't willing to try.

the hardest part about you being gone
isn't just the absence of your company,
it is doing the things that were ours,
doing the things we said we'd do together
without you.

i wish we could go back in time.
but yet again,
there is a reality where,
maybe,
just maybe,
it works.

and it is ten times as beautiful.

and if not,
our separate journeys will account
for the potentialities of the stories
we would've written together.

i remember when i lost you,
i felt as though i was staring into a mirror
without being met back with a reflection.

-my other half

yet no matter how hard i try to forget you,
i know that it's always been you.

our "almost" will forever haunt me

-it was my fault.

there is no one in my life who doesn't know your name,
yet i don't think
any of them,
no matter how long the story,
will truly
know you,
in the manner i did.

i hate that i have to let you go.
you went from being
my favourite future,
to my favourite memory.

i'll forever be sorry that as a person you loved,
i made you feel as though
i didn't want what was best for you.

i prioritised my happiness,
assuming that what was mine
must've been yours.

i had kept running away from the darkness
until i realised
that in it,
we would find our paths to freedom.

i hope to grow in the shade,
to one day,
eventually be enough for
both you and i.

i knew our love was dangerous,
but i didn't know that it'd only
turn to poison in your absence.

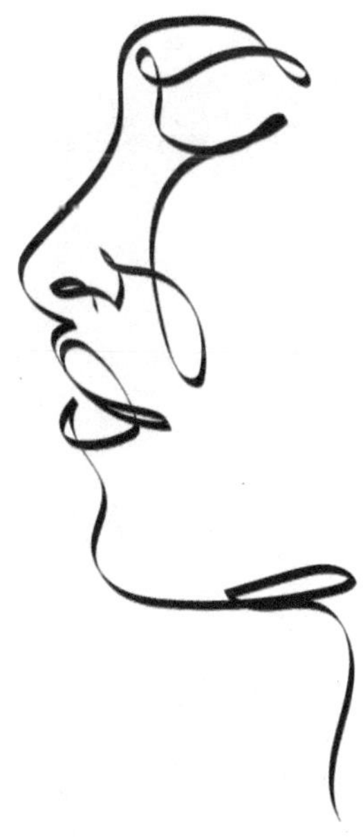

i remember the night we danced under the night sky
it was as if time had stopped.
in that moment it only felt it was
you and i
against the world.

i wish we had more time.

lie and tell me you love me.

-it's not like you haven't before

i hate that i am starting to miss you
more than i can remember you

i despise falling asleep.
for it is when i am not consciously
avoiding the thought of you.

i find myself smiling,
for i am dreaming of you.

i often pray i never wake up,
so i am stuck in the one reality
where it worked out.
the reality where,
we worked out.

i know you said it was impossible,
but i often ponder as to
what magical concoction of words
would've made you stay.

i sometimes wish i could exist
without thinking my sole purpose
is to figure out how to exist without you.

moving on translates to accepting our fate as strangers
i don't think i'm ready for that
and for that i reason
i will continue to write
till the feeling within my fingers suffice.

only then will i love you in silence.

the man who said he'd make my life hell by loving me
shall stand forever corrected.
for he made my life hell
by leaving.

well, maybe truancy is the purest form of love.
i am yet to find out.

teach me how to forget about you
the way you forgot about me.

i had never thought
i'd beg anyone to stay
but the day you left
i found myself begging the universe
if it could somehow hear me

to give me a chance
a chance to once again see you
to once more feel your touch
to one last time feel your breath on my skin.

it was when
when i was on the verge
of losing you
how much i wished i had shown you
how much i loved you
every second of every day.

and for how i wished i hadn't taken for granted
as many moments as i did.

i often sit in silence,
reflecting upon the two questions my mind is willing to piece together.

"what could i have changed?"

"should i have left you alone?"

one of my biggest fears
is that you will realise it was meant to be us
when it's too late.

yet i also fear that i may realise that i remained in love
with you
when i could've fallen for so many other things.

“is that it?”
was that really the end?

with 3 words,
and 8 letters,
there is nothing more i can pray for
but a happier ending.

only the stars know,
how often i
say your name
while you're away.

perhaps we wanted it so badly
and that was why it didn't work

reflection

i saw forever in your eyes
everyday i still question
if forever meant
forever apart,
or together.

i would recognize you in every lifetime,
every universe,
every heaven,
no matter what entity your soul may possess.

and i promise you that my love
would remain identical
to that of my infatuation in this lifetime.

why, you may ask?
because i knew
from the second i met you
that it was you,
and i knew that it would be you
in each lifetime and the next.

i fell for you
forgetting the simplicity
of knowing that i breathe within pages
i do not scribe.

i felt so safe with you.
it was if your arms were walls
protecting me from the trenches
of the outside world.

it was as if time didn't exist when i was with you.

i remember when i first realised i loved you,
i couldn't imagine loving you more
than i did in that present moment,
although i knew i would the next day
and the days after that,
till eternity to come.

the day you left i prayed
that each part of me
that loved you
would eventually disappear
into the abyss of oblivion,
yet i stand today loving you more
than i ever have
knowing that i will only love you more
as the days go by,

to the next day and the days after that,
till eternity to come.

for me home was the boy
who understood me
as the sun did the moon.

it was him
who made the bad days good,

who'd paint the sky blue
when it felt even a hint of grey,

who'd drown himself in the rain
to simply hold an umbrella over my head.

you ask me why i loved you,
how could i have not?
you were everything
i ever wanted,
everything i ever needed.

it was the day i met you
when it felt as though,
my soul had found
what it'd been searching for
since the beginning.

i often find myself filling my ego,
with hoaxed confidence,
often telling myself
"there will be many more
people i am yet to love."

it's not that i have come to disagree
with that sentiment,

yet everyday that goes by
i realise that genuine love only occurs
once in a blue moon.

and you have been my favourite azure
since the day that i met you.

him and i often spoke on what we'd do
if we ever lost one other.

whatever words came out of my mouth
fell astray from my mind.

for the only thought that settled was,
"find him. if i were to ever lose him, all i'd ever want to do is to find him."

i wasn't devoid of emotion,
rather i chose to stay numb.

but when we were together
you taught me that emotions
were so intricately beautiful,
even if that emotion
was perpetual pain.

whether across the room
or on the moon.
i'd still miss you.

my heart does not know distance.

i often think about how they're people that have phased this earth,
who've had you before me,
yet still weren't willing to give you the world.
idiocy at its finest.

although it may not have meant much to you,
i still think about us,
during every glimpse i take of the limelight
that shines within our shared empyrean.

i constantly whisper,
to the god above,
if he may hear me,
to answer my one wish,
to let me love you more than i will ever gain.

for those were the moments where i was happiest.
loving you.
being with you.

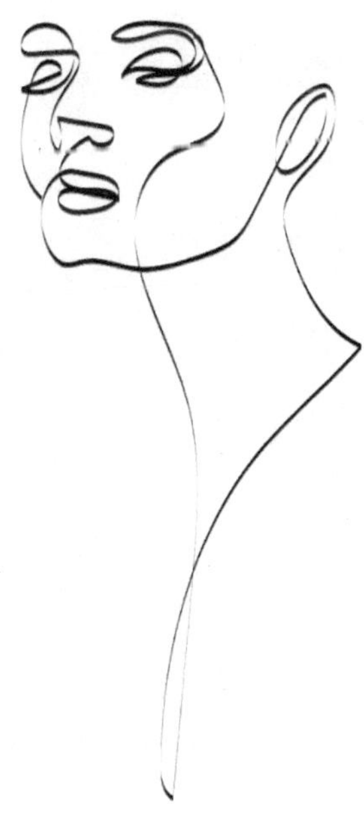

i still find it unbelievable
how quickly
we went from
everything
to nothing.

meant to be, yet not meant to last.
at least at that moment in time.

i'd rather live with the pain of waiting
than with a life of regret
knowing our story ended with "what if?"

and with you
the world would go silent.

you reminded me i was with soul.

even the most painful moments with him,
were infinitely better than the
"perfect" moments
with others

you made me forget what the days without you felt like.

when i was with you
i felt like i was forever stuck in the loop
of the best part of my favourite song

-i now understand why forever is a word meant for memories not people

how is it that emptiness feels so heavy?

maybe you wouldn't seem like a monster
in your own eyes
if you could see yourself through the
eyes that struggled to find a flaw in you.

it was not that
we failed to communicate
with one another
we failed to understand.

oceans of voices,
yet i remain searching for yours.

"you've survived too many storms to be bothered by raindrops,"
although
it was the same rain that appeared so beautiful
that drowned me.
whether it was a tsunami or a mere droplet.

if i were to be in a room with everyone i ever loved
i would run to you,
yet i still question whether you would catch me.

i can't afford to lose the few tomorrows i have
thinking about you,
for that is how i spent all my yesterdays.
yet how do i go by,
as you were all that i had known.

i find myself missing you most
in the future that we planned

you made me want to try.

art has always had a way of speaking to my soul
and you will forever be my favourite piece

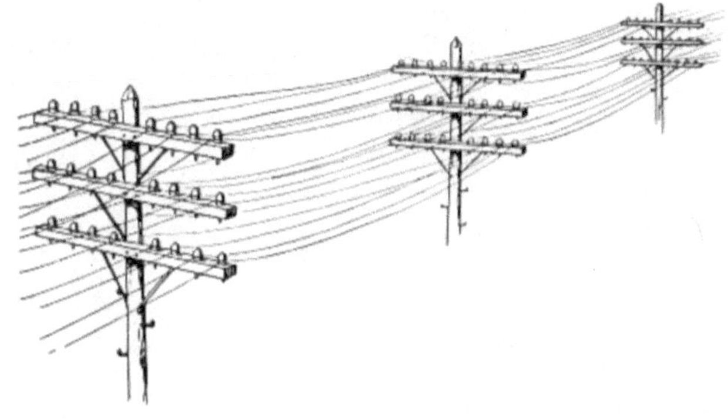

you smiled and suddenly
i forgot my worries of tomorrow
and the days after.

i realised that love is a choice.
and you didn't choose me.
and that's okay.

-i wouldn't have had to beg for you to stay if i was what you wanted.

maybe i was simply there to push you forward while i stayed behind finding my own path.

burdened by the thoughts of us
i never had the time
to figure out
what it felt like to hear my own.

you tell me you no longer love me,
yet,
i remember the nights you'd call me "beautiful" as if it were my name.

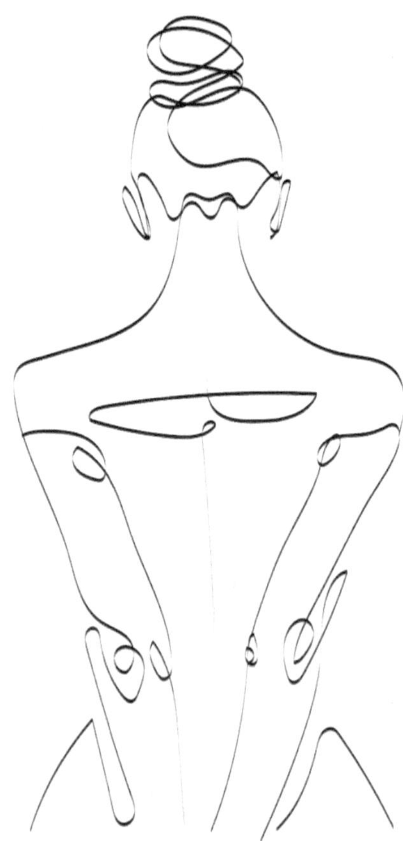

acceptance

knowing one person in the world
knew how crazy in love
i was with you,
and smiled
thinking about it,

will forever be enough of a reason
to remain fulfilled with
the story we left behind.

we never stood a chance,
i knew that since the second i met you,
but when i was with you,
i almost didn't care.

we were both young
learning how to be good people.

how could we have known right from wrong?

in another life we'll be laughing at the possibility that we didn't work in other lifetimes.

i remain painting the flowers i had crafted for you.

whenever i feel lost
i look to the sky
knowing that the limelight of the moon
is always there,
hence
i am always home

what hurt most was that,
you were also my best friend.

and as silly as it is,
you still are
even through your absence.

there many things that i have done
that i rue deeply.

but i simply cannot regret
the choices, the disarray, the affliction,
that brought me to you.

a sight i'd walk through hell
to merely witness once again.

if god doesn't bless me with success in this lifetime
i will spend my lifetime of prayers,
hoping that he is to bless you with the success
i failed to earn.

waiting
doesn't simply translate to
'waiting for you to love me.'
but being patient towards
becoming the person i've never been before,
in the best way possible.

for our love is not promised.

-i will never know how far i can go by staying to the very inch of where i am right now.

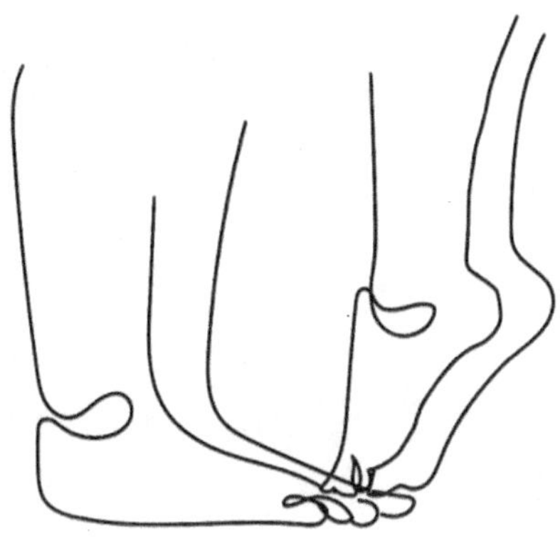

choosing me over you
felt like watching myself become a villain
in the eyes i fell in love with.
yet i realise
that this is all you would've ever wanted
even if it came at the cost of betraying,
my favourite part of me,
you.

begging you to stay
was the equivalent of licking the
remaining drops of love
you had left for me
off of knives.

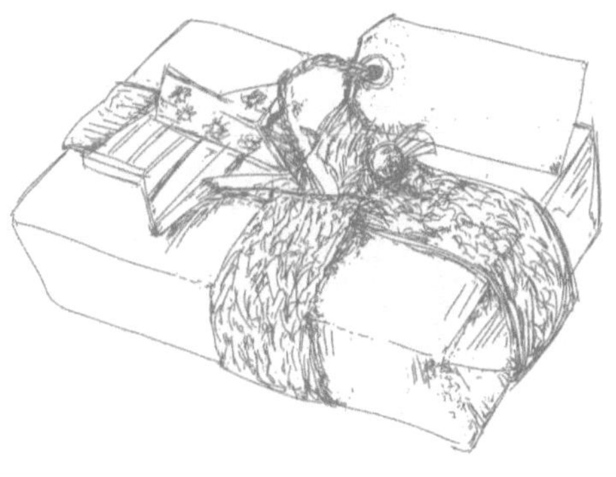

knowing tomorrow's sun will rise the same
i will not change the intentions i hold
for misery has become my comfort

eventually i came to realise my own value
and loved the girl that had been with me all along.
for often the people who are hardest to love,
are the ones who needed the love most after all.

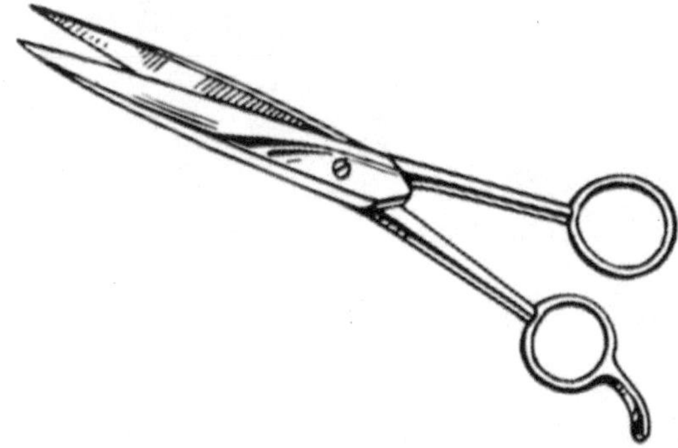

the door is still open.
i simply am no longer there holding it.

although,
i will forever be waiting on the other side
even if you simply wish to
come and say hi.

i hope that when the beautiful things
that are destined for you
occur,
you believe you are worthy of all it,
and the rest of the miracles
meant for you.

"loving him unconditionally
will not make him love you."

-words i wish heard

how silly of me
to have forgotten
that *i*
am the love of my life?

much of me wishes the clock stopped
the moment we fell in love
but without us coming to an end,
i would have never found me.

praying for you is my love language
not a conversation with god goes by
without the mention of your name.

i think the most beautiful part of loving you
was falling in love with the girl you first met,
and giving her love that she deserved.

"if in this lifetime
i am to fail to find a love that imitates a mere fraction
of the infatuation i shared with him.
may you leave me lone
and guide my soul to his or the one made for me in the
afterlife
for i will never fulfil the love one deserves
for my heart belongs to another."

-my last prayer

most of the time i had spent,
wishing to disappear,
all i truly hoped was to
be is found

i wanted to love,
and you wanted to leave.

-and that is okay.

i hope my absence will give you more peace than my love did.

in another life, maybe i will have the privledge of
being loved by you for a lifetime.

how can i kill myself for another,
when i'm *still dying* for you?

www.ingramcontent.com/pod-product-compliance
Lightning Source LLC
LaVergne TN
LVHW041116150826
845673LV00007B/2080

* 9 7 9 8 8 9 2 7 7 4 9 4 9 *